THE BRAIN

OUR NERVOUS SYSTEM

SEYMOUR SIMON

A MULBERRY PAPERBACK BOOK
• NEW YORK •

Photography Note

Scientists are using fantastic new machines that peer inside the human body to picture the invisible and help doctors save lives. In this book, we see extraordinary views of the brain and nervous system. Many of these images were taken by various kinds of scanners, which change X-ray photos into computer code to make clear, colorful graphics. The computer-enhanced pictures of planets beamed back to Earth from distant space use a similar technique. These new ways of seeing help all of us to understand and appreciate that most wonderful machine: the human body.

The author would like to thank Orli R. Etingin, M.D., for her careful reading of the manuscript of this book.

PHOTO AND ART CREDITS

Permission to use the following photographs is gratefully acknowledged: page 5, Alfred Pasieka/Science Photo Library; page 6, Professor P. Motta/Department of Anatomy, University La Sapienza, Rome/Science Photo Library; page 7, VU/John D. Cunningham; page 8, VU/David M. Phillips; page 11, VU/E. R. Lewis, T. E. Everhart, Y. Y., Zeevi; front cover and pages 15, 19, 24, 32, Scott Camazine; page 16, Dr. Colin Chumbley/Science Photo Library; page 20, Astrid and Hanns-Frieder Michler/Science Photo Library; page 21, VU/Fred Hossler; page 23, CNRI/Science Photo Library; page 27, VU/L. Bassett, Videosurgery; page 28, Hank Morgan; page 31, Dr. M. Phelps and Dr. J. Mazziotta et alia/Neurology/Science Photo Library. Art on page 13 by Ann Neumann.

The text type is 18-point Garamond Book.

The Library of Congress has cataloged the Morrow Junior Books edition of *The Brain* as follows:
Simon, Seymour.
The brain: our nervous system/Seymour Simon.
p. cm.
Summary: Describes the various parts of the brain and the nervous system and how they function to enable us to think, feel, move, and remember.
ISBN 0-688-14640-6 (trade). ISBN 0-688-14641-4 (lib. bdg.)
1. Brain—Juvenile literature. 2. Nervous system—Juvenile literature. [1. Nervous system.] I. Title.
QP365.5.P365 1997 612.8—dc21 96-36801 CIP AC

1 3 5 7 9 10 8 6 4 2
First Mulberry Edition, 1999
ISBN 0-688-17060-9

To Robert, Nicole, Joel,
and Benjamin Simon

Wiggle your toes. Scratch your nose. Take a deep breath and yawn. Decide which is your favorite food. Try to remember the last time you ate it. Count the number of words in this sentence. Think about what you would like to do tomorrow. Then cup your hands around your head and feel the bones of your skull. Inside your skull is your brain. Your brain is the control center for everything you do.

Each second, millions of signals pass through your brain, carrying all kinds of messages. They bring news about what your body is doing and feeling. Your brain examines the messages, produces thoughts and memories, then plans what to do next. Signals go out from your brain to other parts of your body to enable you to read, run, laugh, breathe, say hello to a friend, or turn to the next page in this book. Try it!

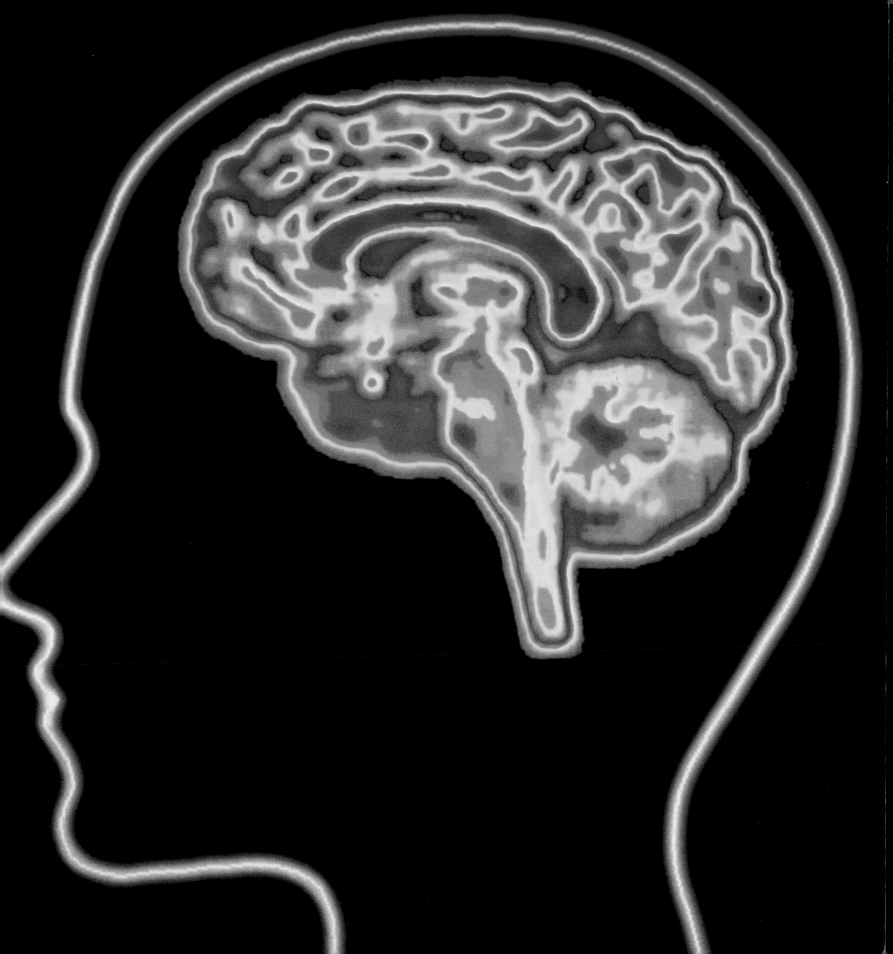

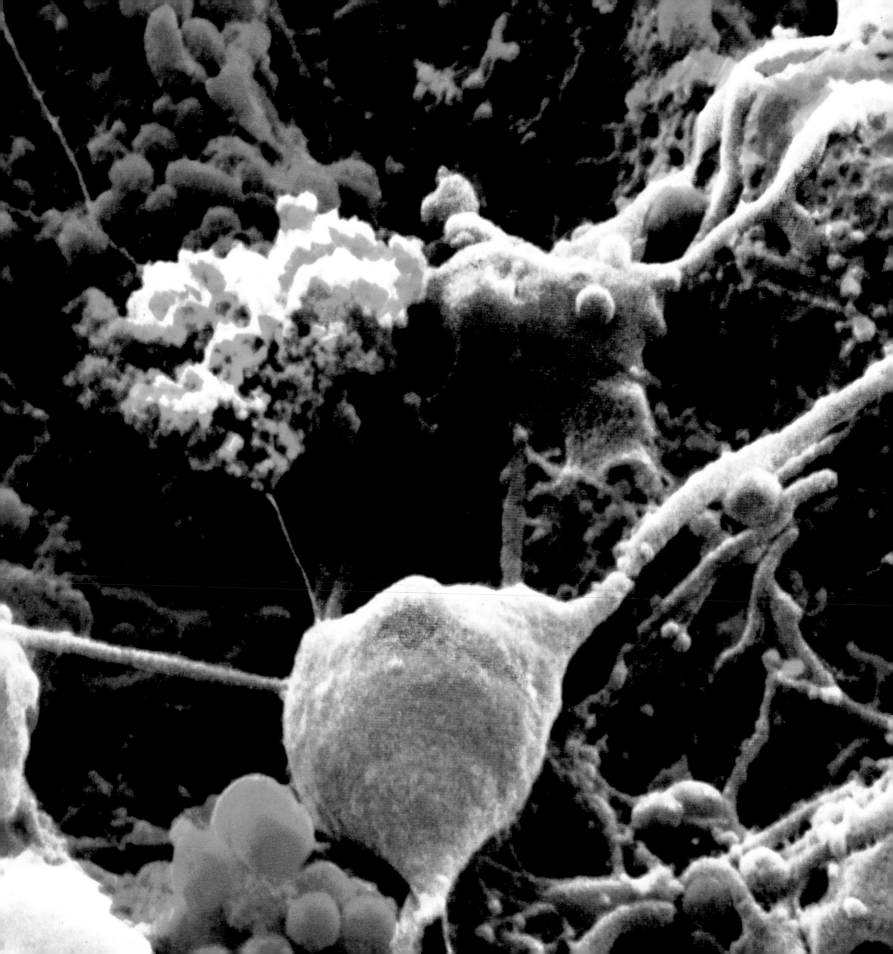

Your brain, like the rest of your body, is made up of hundreds of billions of microscopic cells. Many of them are special messenger cells called neurons. Neurons carry signals back and forth from the brain to other parts of your body.

Billions upon billions of neurons are linked throughout your body in networks that make up the two main parts of your nervous system. The central nervous system, or CNS, consists of your brain and spinal cord. The network of nerves outside your brain is called the peripheral nervous system, or PNS.

Glial cells in the brain outnumber the neurons ten to one. Glial cells do not carry messages. They support the neurons by supplying nutrients and other chemicals, repairing the brain after an injury, and attacking invading bacteria.

This computer-colored micrograph taken by a scanning electron microscope (SEM) shows neurons (grayish white) and glial cells (red-orange), magnified over 20,000 times.

A bundle of neurons is called a nerve. Nerves are the body's wiring. They carry tiny electrical-chemical signals called nerve impulses. Nerves branch out from the brain and spinal cord to your eyes and ears, your stomach, skin, bones, and even inside your teeth. The thinnest nerves are narrower than a hair. The thickest nerves look like pieces of white rope.

A single nerve cell has a central cell body, branching threads called dendrites, and a long wirelike axon. The dendrites carry electrical signals toward the cell body, while the axon carries the signal away.

Axons are thinner than the thinnest hair, but some axons reach from the spinal cord to the feet. Axons are often surrounded by a fatty covering called a myelin sheath. Myelin acts like insulation around an electric wire and helps speed nerve messages.

Neurons' cell bodies, dendrites, and axons are revealed in these highly magnified computer-colored SEMs.

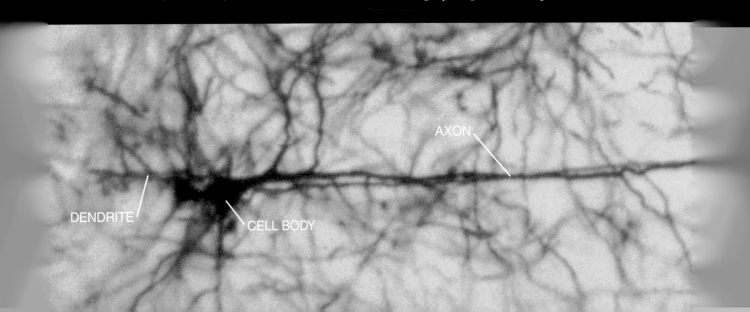

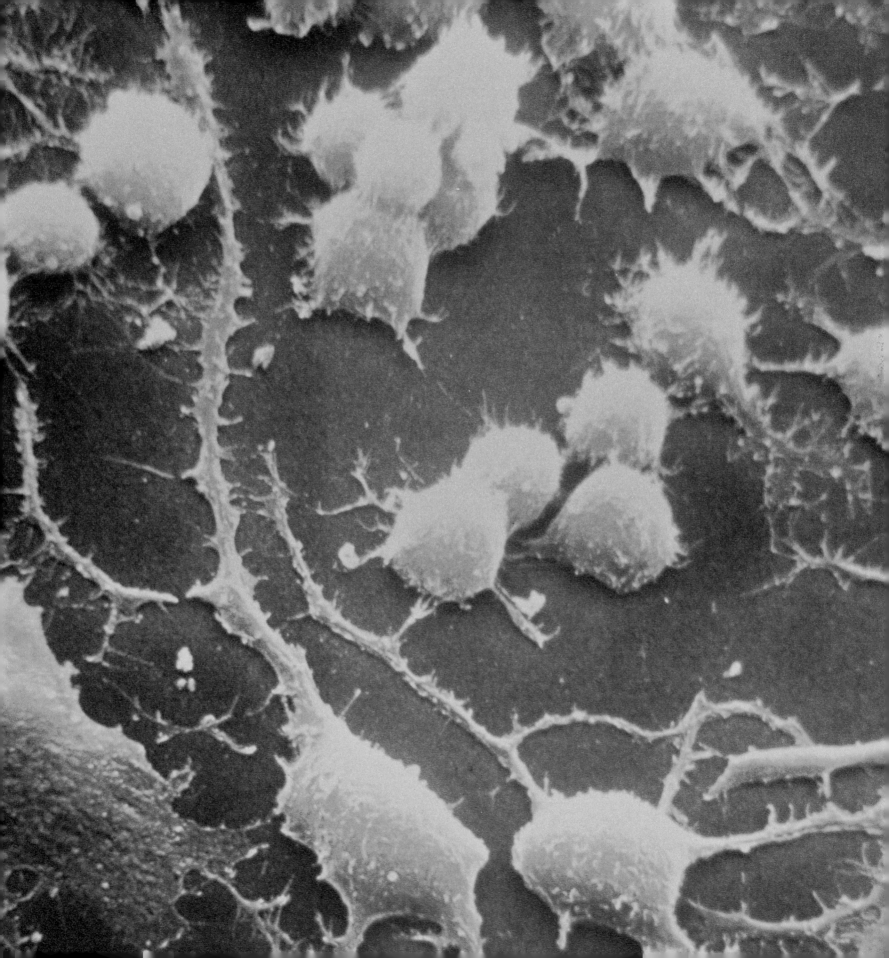

Because nerves don't touch one another, a message has to leap from one to the next across a tiny gap called a synapse. A synapse is about a millionth of an inch wide and is a kind of living switch.

When an electrical impulse reaches the knobby ends of an axon, it triggers the release of a chemical. This instantly jumps across the synapse to dendrites on the next nerve cell. The chemical causes the dendrites to trigger an electrical signal. The message continues through the cell body to the end of the axon, where it is passed from one neuron to many others along an almost endless number of pathways. Synapses always pass signals in the same direction; they cannot work in reverse.

The knobby ends of axons are seen in this highly magnified computer-colored SEM.

When you touch something hot, your brain tells you how hot it is. But how did your brain find out? Let's follow a single message as it moves through millions of nerve cells from your finger to your brain.

A stimulus is something that makes a nerve cell fire off a message called a response. There are all kinds of stimuli, including touch, sound, light, taste, temperature, and smell. Nerve cells that respond to stimuli are called sensory neurons. Your skin has millions of sensory neurons. A single touch may make thousands of them respond.

When your finger touches something hot, signals from touch sensors in your skin travel along sensory nerves at speeds of up to four hundred feet a second. In a split second, the signals reach relay nerves in your spinal cord and then transfer to other nerves that go to your brain, which "feels" the touch. Your brain then sends out messages to your spinal cord and then to motor nerves. Motor nerves carry messages to muscle cells that make your arm move.

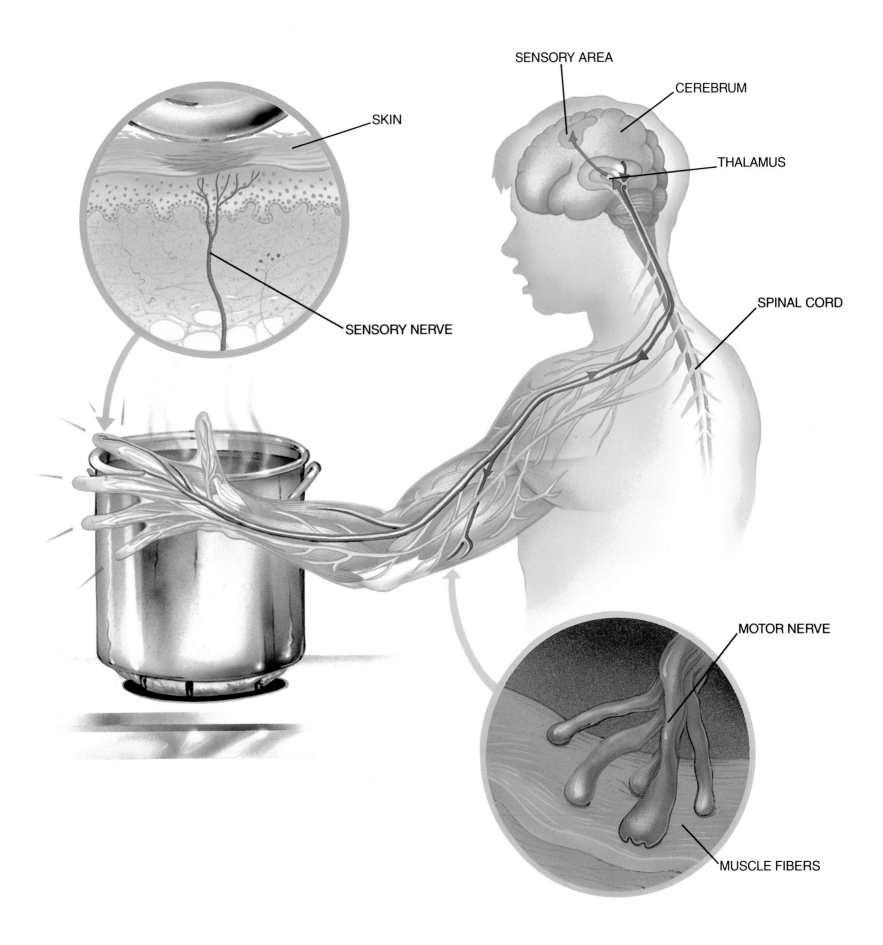

SENSORY AREA

CEREBRUM

THALAMUS

SKIN

SPINAL CORD

SENSORY NERVE

MOTOR NERVE

MUSCLE FIBERS

Your skull is made up of twenty-eight bones. Eight of the bones fit together like pieces of a jigsaw puzzle. They form a strong eggshell shape that protects the brain. These bones make up your braincase, or cranium. The other twenty bones help shape your jaws and face.

Inside the skull, the brain sits in a liquid bath that helps protect and cushion it against shocks. A human brain is about the size of a large grapefruit and weighs about three pounds when fully grown. It looks like a wrinkled blob of pinkish gray jelly. Many blood vessels run through the brain. They bring oxygen, water, and dissolved food that the brain constantly needs to function.

At birth, the cranium is not fully formed. Your brain continues to grow in size until you are seven years old. The human brain is not the biggest brain among animals; a whale's is much larger. But a human brain is the biggest compared to body size.

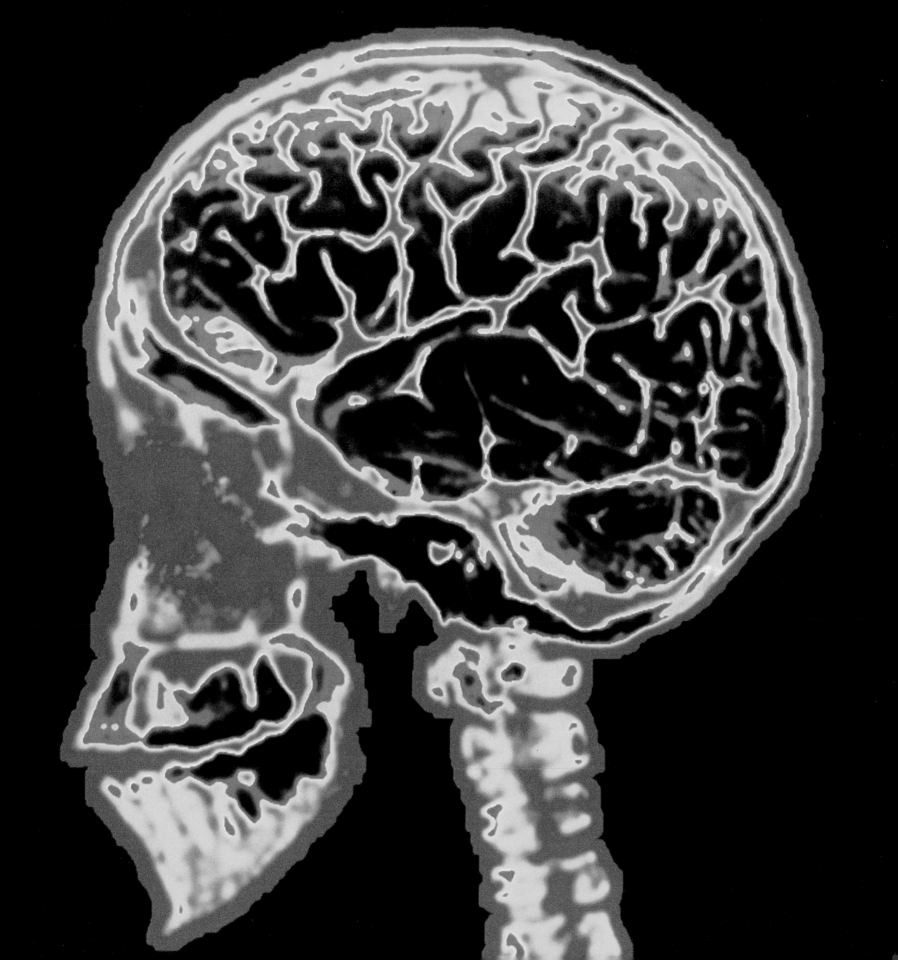

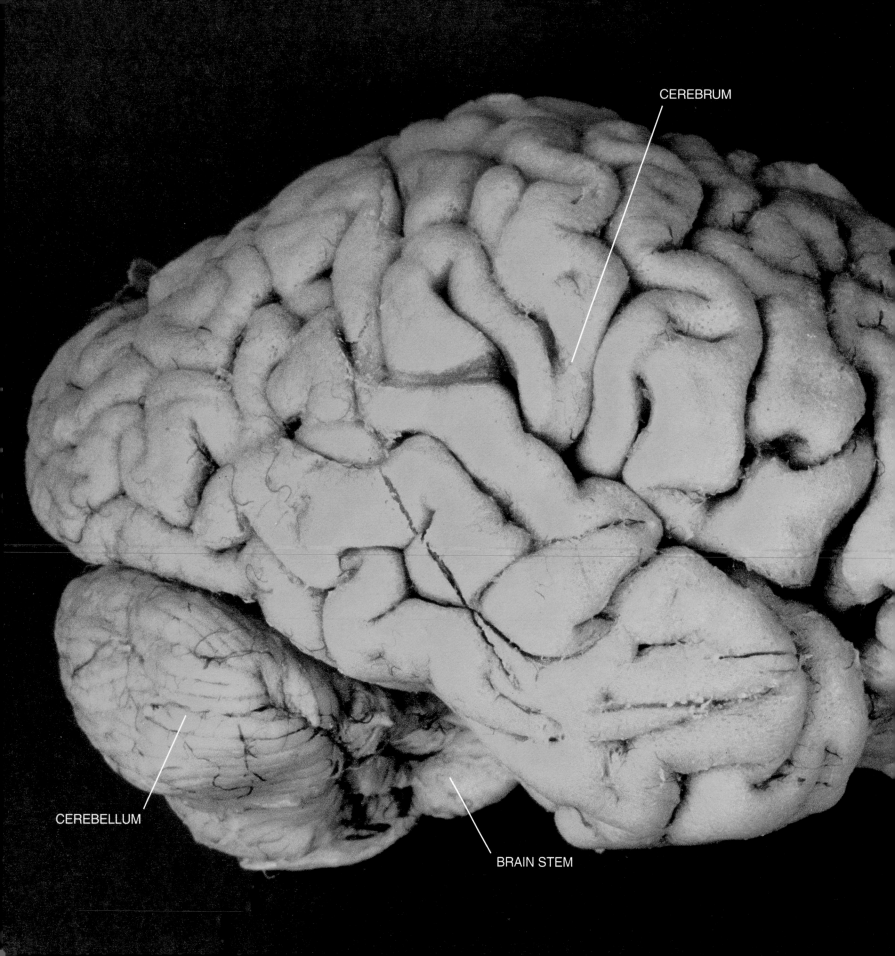

CEREBRUM

CEREBELLUM

BRAIN STEM

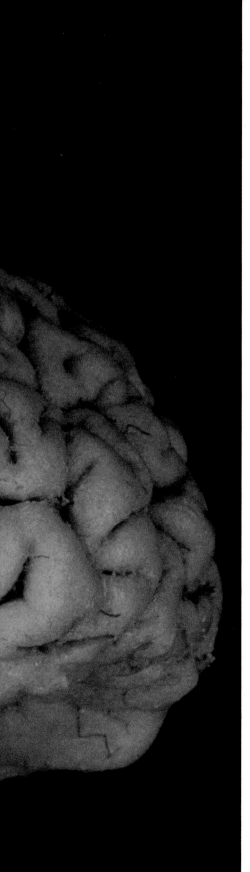

The brain has three main sections: the cerebrum, the cerebellum, and the brain stem. The cerebrum fills the whole upper part of the skull, about nine-tenths of a person's whole brain. *Cerebrum* comes from a Latin word that means "brain." The cerebrum is divided into four parts, called lobes. This is the "thinking brain," in which language, memory, sensations, and decision making are located.

The deeply wrinkled gray surface of the cerebrum is called the cerebral cortex. The cortex is about as thick as a piece of cardboard, and if it was flattened out, it would take up as much space as the top of a kitchen table. The cortex is made up of ten to fourteen *billion* neurons. That's many more neurons than there are people in the entire world.

The cerebral cortex is working every time you listen to music, taste an apple, play with a computer, or make some part of your body move.

The cerebrum and its cortex are divided down the middle from front to back into two halves, called the right and the left cerebral hemispheres. The two hemispheres are linked to each other by a thick bundle of nerves.

Each hemisphere controls the muscles of the opposite side of the body. In most people, one side becomes more developed than the other side. If you usually kick with your right foot and point with your right hand, then your left hemisphere is in control. But if you usually use your left foot and left hand, your right hemisphere is dominant.

The left hemisphere generally controls the ability to read, speak, and do mathematical problems. The right hemisphere is the center of musical and artistic creation and the ability to understand shape and form—even to have a sense of humor.

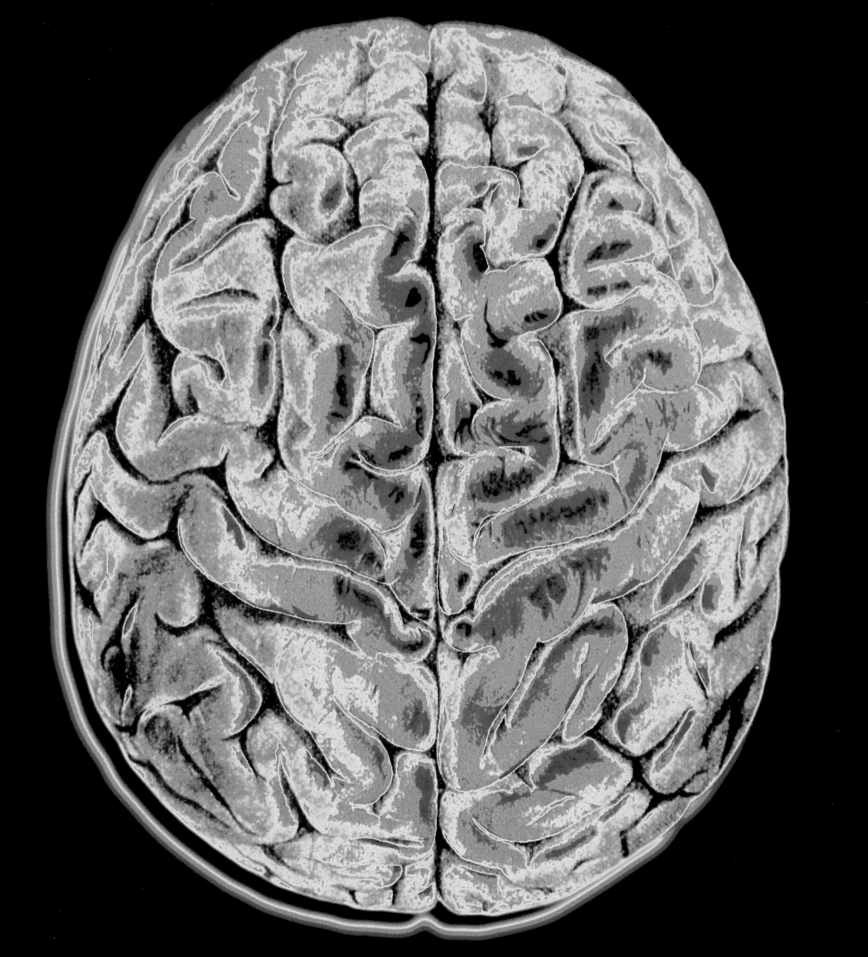

The word *cerebellum* means "little brain," and it looks like a smaller version of the cerebrum. It's tucked underneath the cerebral hemispheres, and it also has two hemispheres that are connected to each other by a thick band of nerves. Other nerves connect the cerebellum to the rest of your brain.

The cerebellum is the brain center for muscle movement, posture, and coordination. The cerebellum is the part of your brain that lets you drink water without spilling it, walk or run easily, and throw a ball straight. It constantly receives messages about the body's actions and position, then sends back commands to the muscles, adjusting the way the body moves.

This photo—taken through a light microscope—shows neuron pathways in the cerebellum magnified hundreds of times.

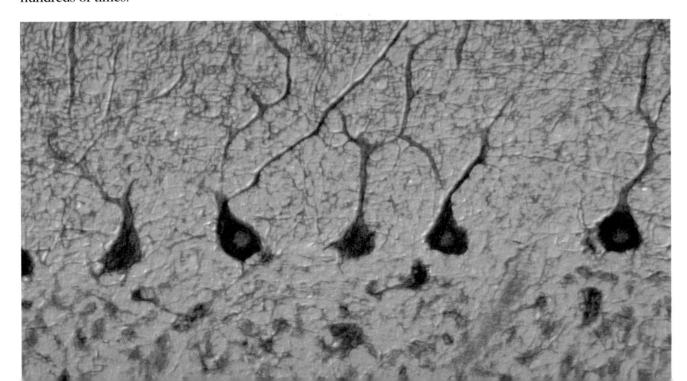

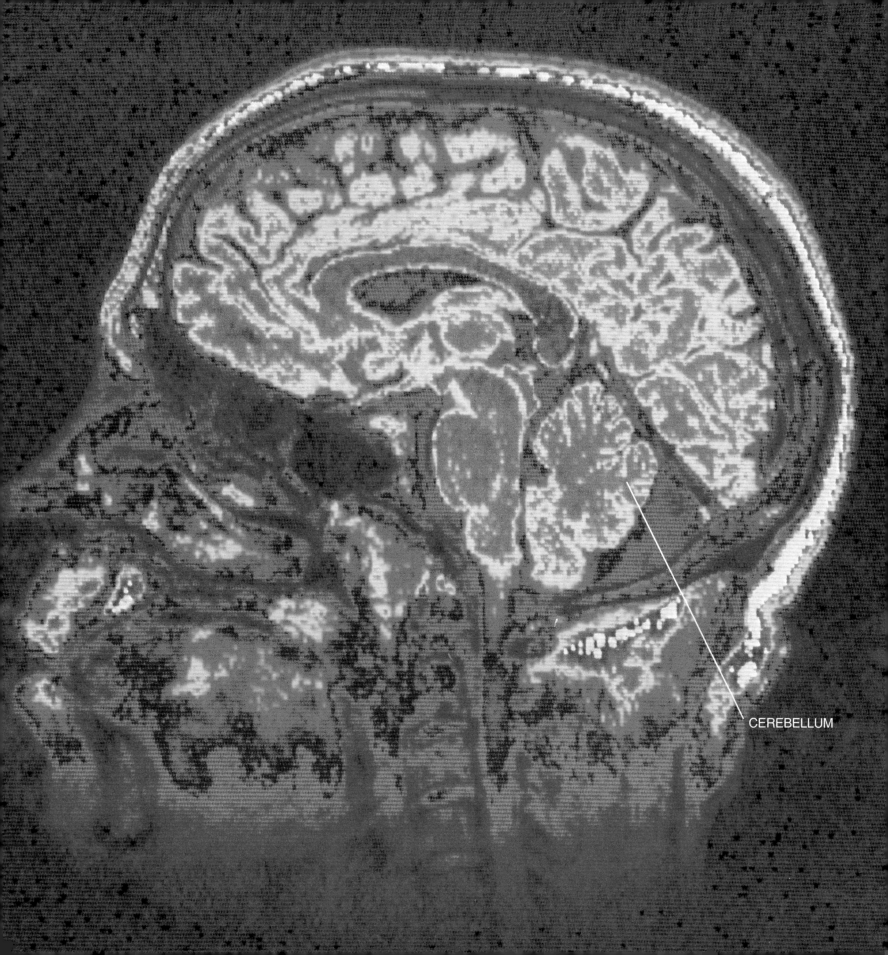

CEREBELLUM

Deep inside and between the two cerebral hemispheres are the thalamus and the hypothalamus. *Thalamus* means "inner room" in Latin. It is a kind of relay station between your spinal cord and your cerebrum. The thalamus is the place that first receives messages signaling such sensations as pain, pressure, and temperature from sensory neurons. The messages are then relayed to the cerebrum. Outgoing motor signals from the cerebral cortex are also first sent to the thalamus. They then travel to the spinal cord and to motor neurons in muscles. Your sense receptors for taste, touch, sight, and sound send messages into the thalamus as the first stop in your brain.

The hypothalamus is just below the thalamus. *Hypo* means "under," so *hypothalamus* means "under the inner room." It is about the size of a small bean and is only 1/300 of the weight of the whole brain. Though small, the hypothalamus is an important central monitor for many functions. The hypothalamus helps to keep your body temperature at about 98.6° Fahrenheit no matter how hot or cold it is outside. It is the part of your brain that makes you feel hungry, thirsty, sleepy, angry, afraid, or happy. The hypothalamus also controls the pituitary, or "master gland," which regulates growth and other important processes in the body.

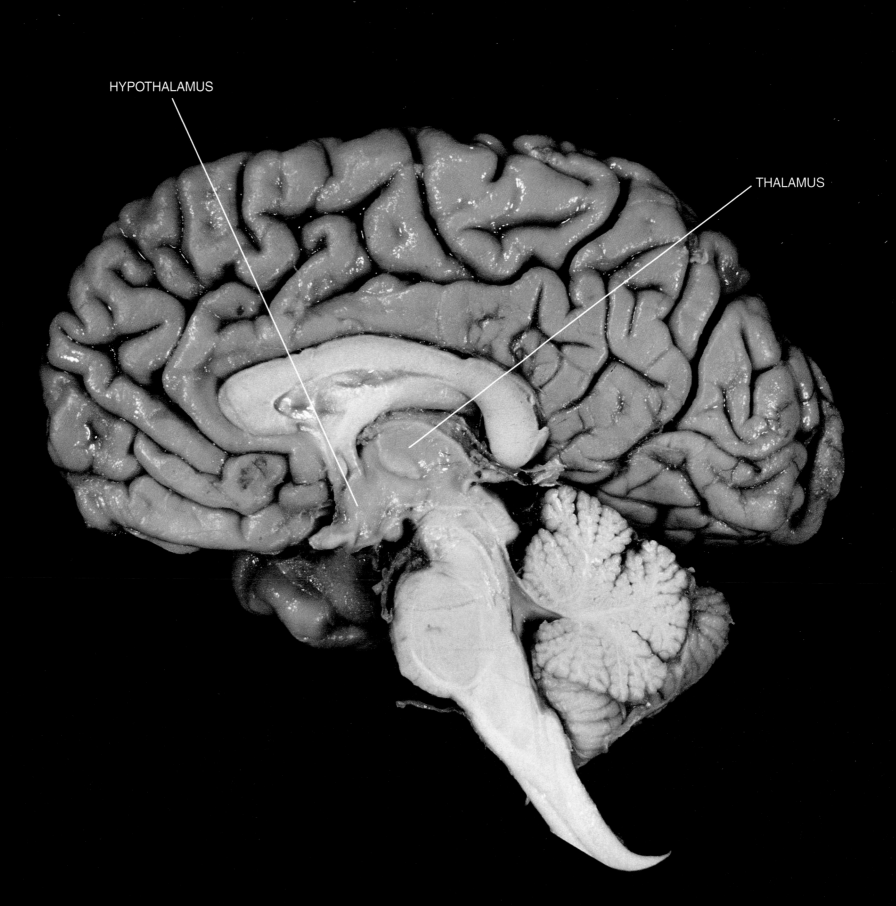

HYPOTHALAMUS

THALAMUS

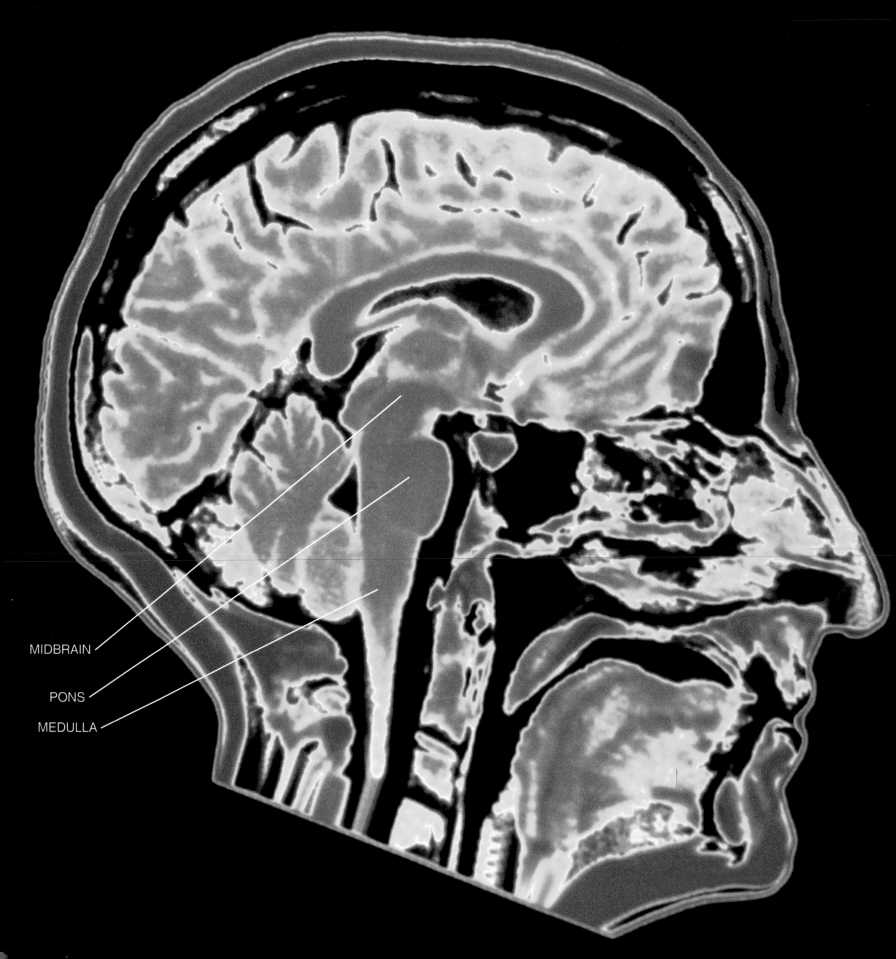

MIDBRAIN

PONS

MEDULLA

The brain stem is the part of the brain that lies below the thalamus and the hypothalamus. It is about three inches long and as thick as your thumb. The brain stem is made up of the midbrain, pons, and medulla.

Highest on the brain stem is the midbrain, which adjusts the sensitivities of your eyes to light and of your ears to sound. Below the midbrain is the pons, which means "bridge." The pons relays messages between the brain and the spinal cord. The one-inch-long medulla blends into the top of the spinal cord. It regulates many of the important automatic functions of your body. These are things you do not think about, such as your heartbeat, blood pressure, digestion, breathing, and swallowing.

Quick, simple responses called reflexes work through the brain stem. For example, pulling your hand away from a hot pot is a simple reflex. If you thought about what to do when you felt the pain, you might get a bad burn. So you just jerk your hand away quickly without thinking about it. At the same time, messages reach the higher parts of your brain so that you can say "ouch" and decide how to take care of the burn.

The spinal cord lies below the brain stem, starting out as a thick white rope and ending as a thin thread. It is the main nerve pathway between your brain and the rest of your body. Your spine is made up of thirty-three separate bones called vertebrae. Your spine helps protect your spinal cord from injury.

This photo of a model of the brain and spinal cord shows that spinal nerves branch out between the vertebrae and go to all parts of the body. Each of these thirty-one pairs of spinal nerves contains thousands of sensory and motor neurons. It is through these neurons that messages travel from the body to the spinal cord and brain and back again.

Horses, dogs, cats, whales, and other mammals have spinal cords and backbones. So do birds, frogs, snakes, and fish. These animals are called vertebrates. Animals without spinal cords and backbones, such as worms and insects, are called invertebrates.

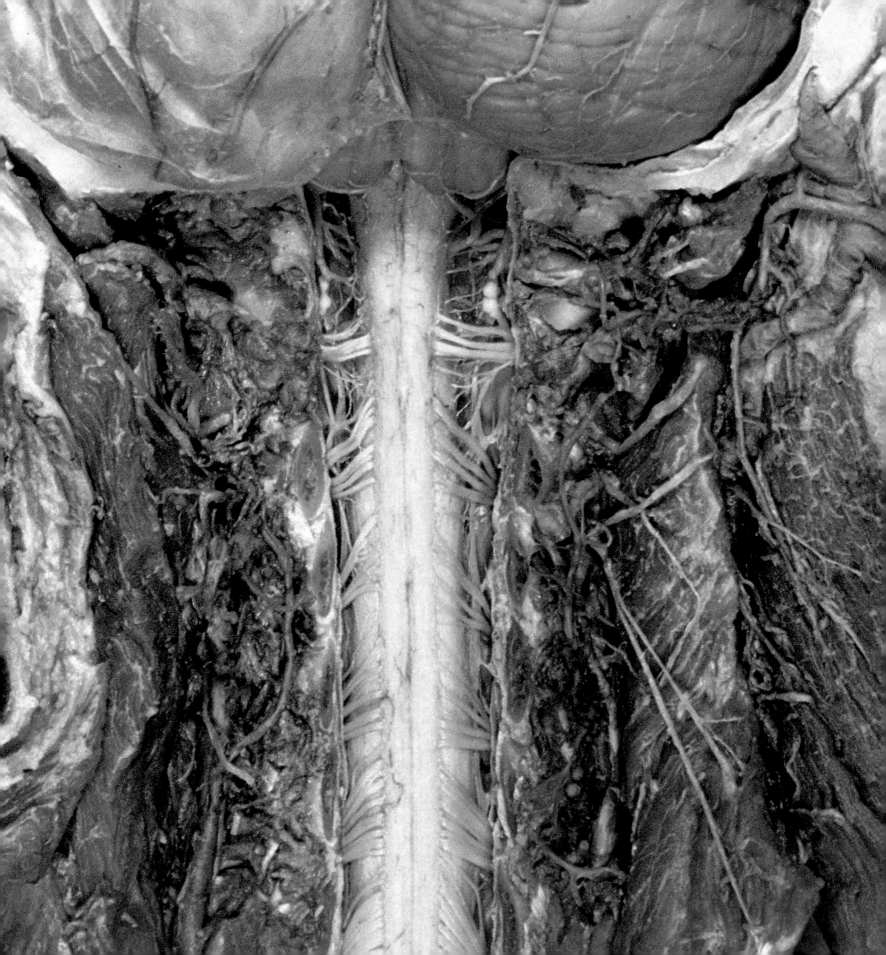

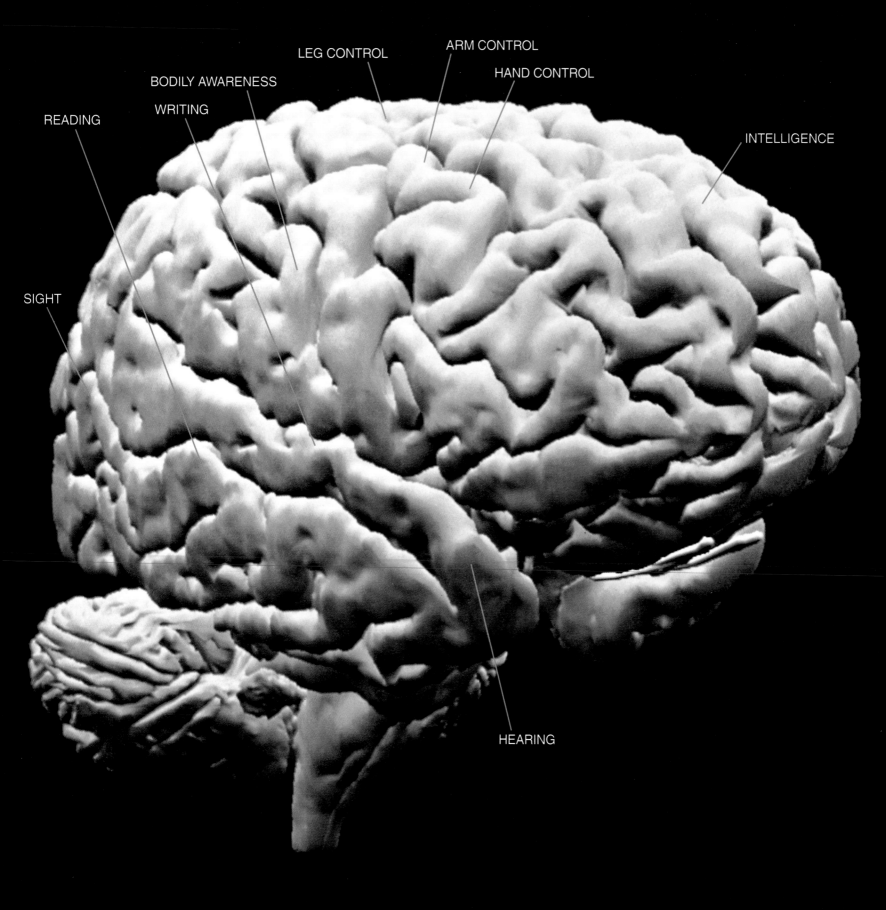

READING

BODILY AWARENESS

WRITING

LEG CONTROL

ARM CONTROL

HAND CONTROL

INTELLIGENCE

SIGHT

HEARING

Can you remember what you had for breakfast this morning? That's called short-term memory. Short-term memory has a very limited time span. You probably can't remember what you had for breakfast two weeks ago. But you can remember some things that happened to you months or even years ago, such as your first day at school. That's called long-term memory.

An area in the front of the cortex seems to deal with short-term memory, while the rest of the cortex deals with both long- and short-term memories. Two narrow motor strips on either side of the cortex control muscles all over your body, such as those in your lips, eyes, neck, thumbs, and so on. Other areas of the cortex receive information from the skin, eyes, ears, nose, and taste buds. Still other areas are related to speech, learning, and thinking.

The actual memories seem to be stored in the chemicals found in nerve cells. One theory is that a change happens in the chemicals that relay nerve impulses. Another idea is that there is a change in the cells' internal chemistry, called RNA. Scientists are just beginning to find out how and where the brain stores memories and where thinking occurs. New discoveries about the brain are constantly being made, but many mysteries still remain.

Sometimes things go wrong with the nervous system. These can range from a brief tension headache to an injury, such as a stroke, that can cause a coma lasting for days or weeks. Injuries to the spinal cord can also be very serious, resulting in partial or complete paralysis.

To find out what is happening in the brain and the nervous system, doctors called neurologists use a device called an electroencephalograph (EEG), which shows electrical activity, or brain waves. Many new techniques help scientists learn how the brain works. CAT scans use X rays to see many layers of brain tissue. MRI scans use magnetic fields to make a picture of a layer of the brain. This positron computed tomography (PCT) photo uses radioactive tracers in blood sugar to show two different levels of visual stimulation in the brain. Note the greater amount of brain activity (in red) when the eyes are open.

VISUAL STIMULATION

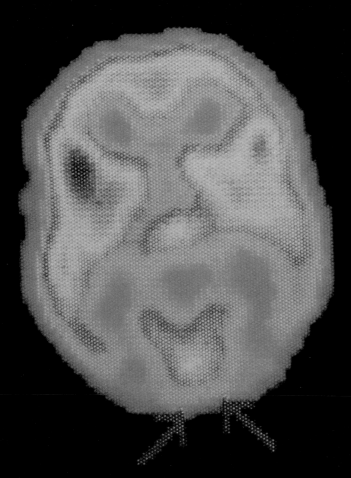

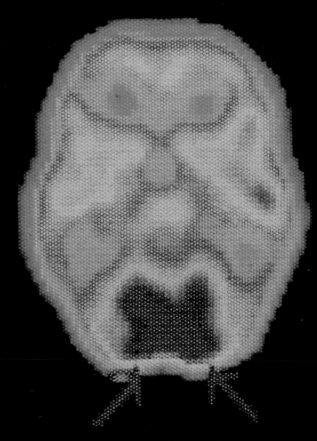

EYES CLOSED

EYES OPENED

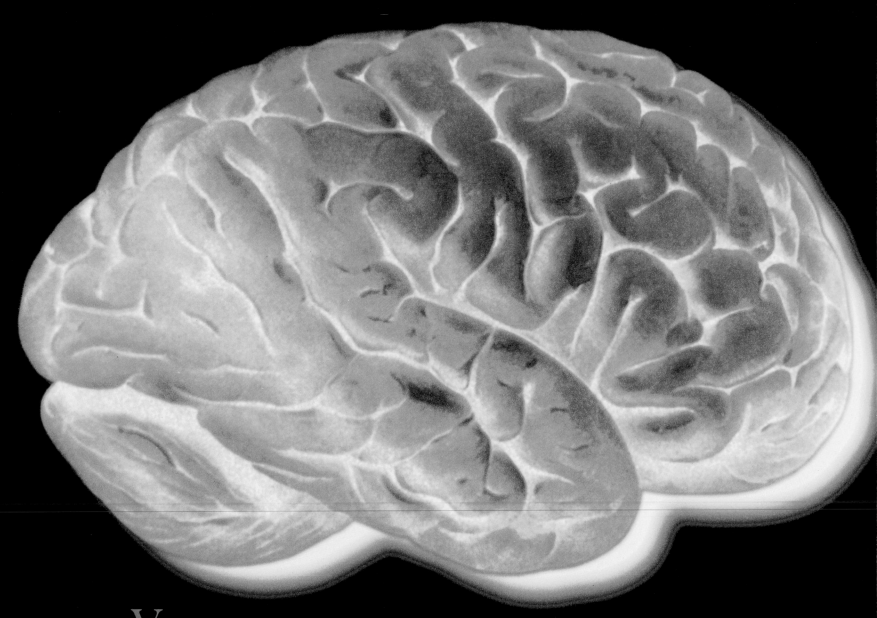

Your brain is only a small part of your whole body. It is not very big, yet it can do more jobs than the most powerful computer ever made. It controls all the other systems of your body and keeps them working smoothly. It is the center of your thoughts, feelings, and memory. Your brain is really what makes you, *you*.